5W's of COVID-19

A Children's Book of Facts

WRITTEN BY DONNA JOHNSON
ILLUSTRATED BY BEVERLY TUNSTALL

Published by True Beginnings Publishing. Copyright Donna Johnson, 2021.

Formatted and Edited by True Beginnings Publishing. Illustrations by Beverly Tunstall. All Illustrations, Cover Art, and text are Copyright Protected.

ISBN-13: 978-1-947082-14-4

Ordering Information:
To order additional copies of this book, please visit Amazon.

5 W's of COVID.
© Donna Johnson.
First Printing, 2021.

Dedication

It is with compassion, understanding, and a spirit of gratitude that I dedicate this labor of love to the countless educators around the globe who went over, above, and beyond for their students. This past year and a half has been nothing no one could have imagined, filled with numerous uncertainties, confusions, discontents, fears, traumas, and despairs, yet the she-roes and heroes of the classroom prevailed. So I salute you all.

What?

6 Feet Apart

Typically in the fall, teachers, administrators, and other school staff are getting ready to open for the new school year. Students are excited, anxious, nervous, and scared. There is a roller coaster of emotions, not just for young students but all ages, even for some teachers. This is usually a happy time for parents. They go shopping with their kids, buying new clothes, school supplies, and much more. Unfortunately, this opening of school would be like none other.

Plexiglass Protection

Schools around the world opened very differently.
Some students are taught on the computer; others
are taught face-to-face while having to wear a mask
and a shield; some having plexiglass placed between
them to separate them from other students and teachers
in the classroom.

Wear A Mask

What we now know about this invisible virus called Covid-19 is that it spreads through talking, sneezing, and coughing. The virus travels through the nose and attacks the lungs and other parts of the body. Anyone can catch this deadly virus no matter the age, race, or gender.

When?

School
Closed

In the spring of 2020, thousands of schools around the world closed because of a virus called Covid-19. Virtual teaching took the place of traditional face-to-face instruction.

No in-person Graduations

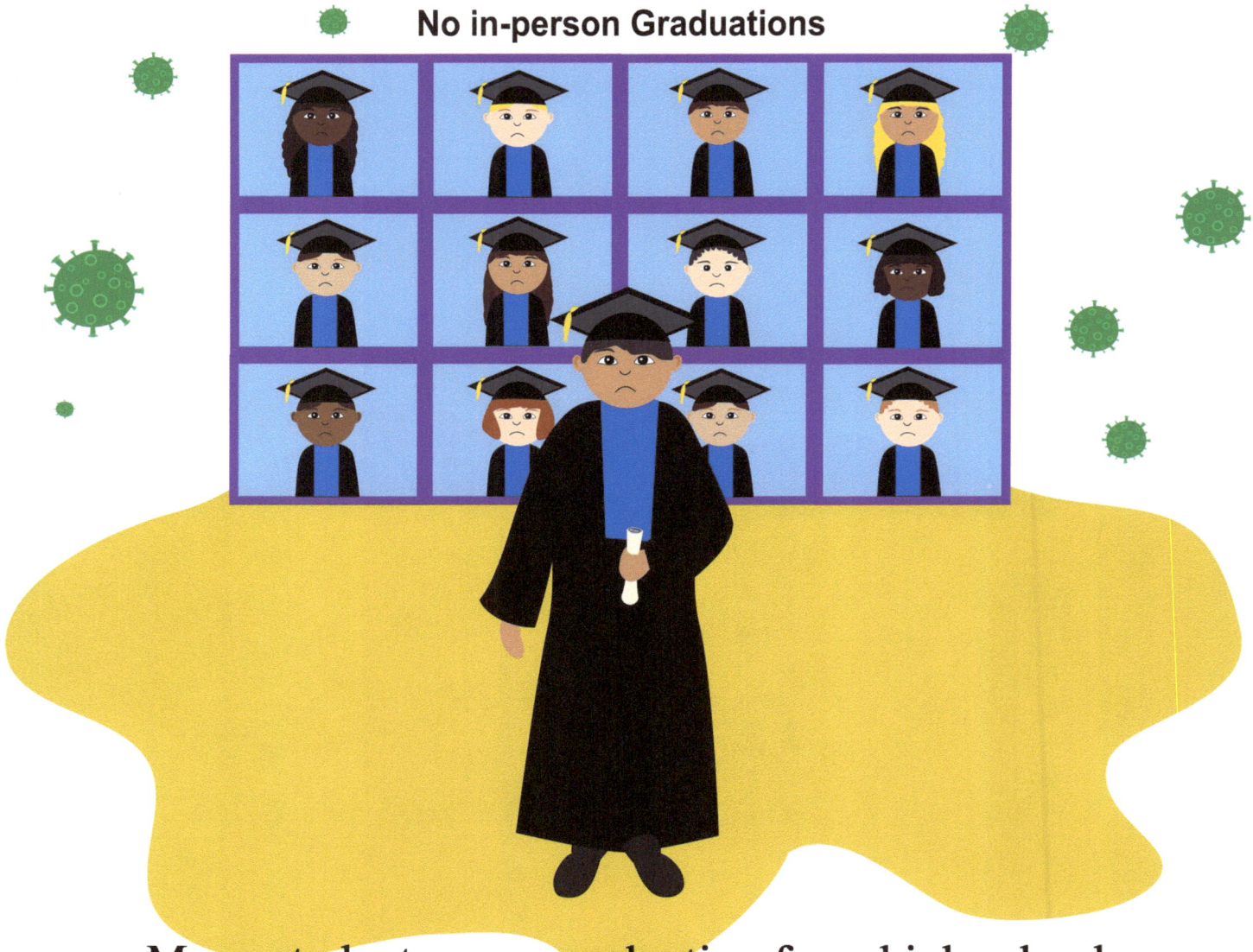

Many students were graduating from high school or going to other grades. These students were not able to celebrate traditional graduation ceremonies or have parties with more than ten people.

Many people also lost jobs and did not know when they would be able to go back to work. Thousands of people died around the world. No one knew when schools would reopen for face-to-face teaching. Life as people knew it before Covid-19 would never be the same.

7

Where?

A Chinese scientist from Wuhan first discovered cases of Covid-19. China became the epicenter of the virus, and although it is located thousands of miles away from the United States, the United Kingdom, Africa, Italy, Australia, and many other countries, that did not stop the virus from spreading.

People traveling on airplanes, boats, trains, and in cars did not know they were spreading the virus all over the world. Social distancing was mandatory, everywhere.

6 Feet Apart

6 Feet Apart

6 Feet Apart

11

Who?

Dr. Anthony Fauci

Dr. Deborah Birx

Everyone around the world has been affected in some way because of this virus. There are scientists and doctors working to discover a cure for Covid-19. Dr. Anthony Fauci and Dr. Deborah Birx are two very important people who work at the White House. Part of their jobs is to tell everyone about the virus and how to stay safe. One source in which they get their information from is the CDC. The CDC is a national public health agency located in the United States for over 60 years. The CDC has been dedicated to protecting health through the prevention and control of disease. Once Dr. Anthony Fauci and Dr. Deborah Birx get new information about the virus, they communicate to everyone what they need to do in order stay safe, as well as what should be done to help stop the spread of Covid-19.

Dr. Kizzmekia Corbett

Another important scientist who has been working to develop a cure for Covid-19 is Dr. Kizzmekia Corbett. Dr. Anthony Fauci spotlighted Dr. Kizzmekia Corbett at the forefront of the Covid-19 vaccine.

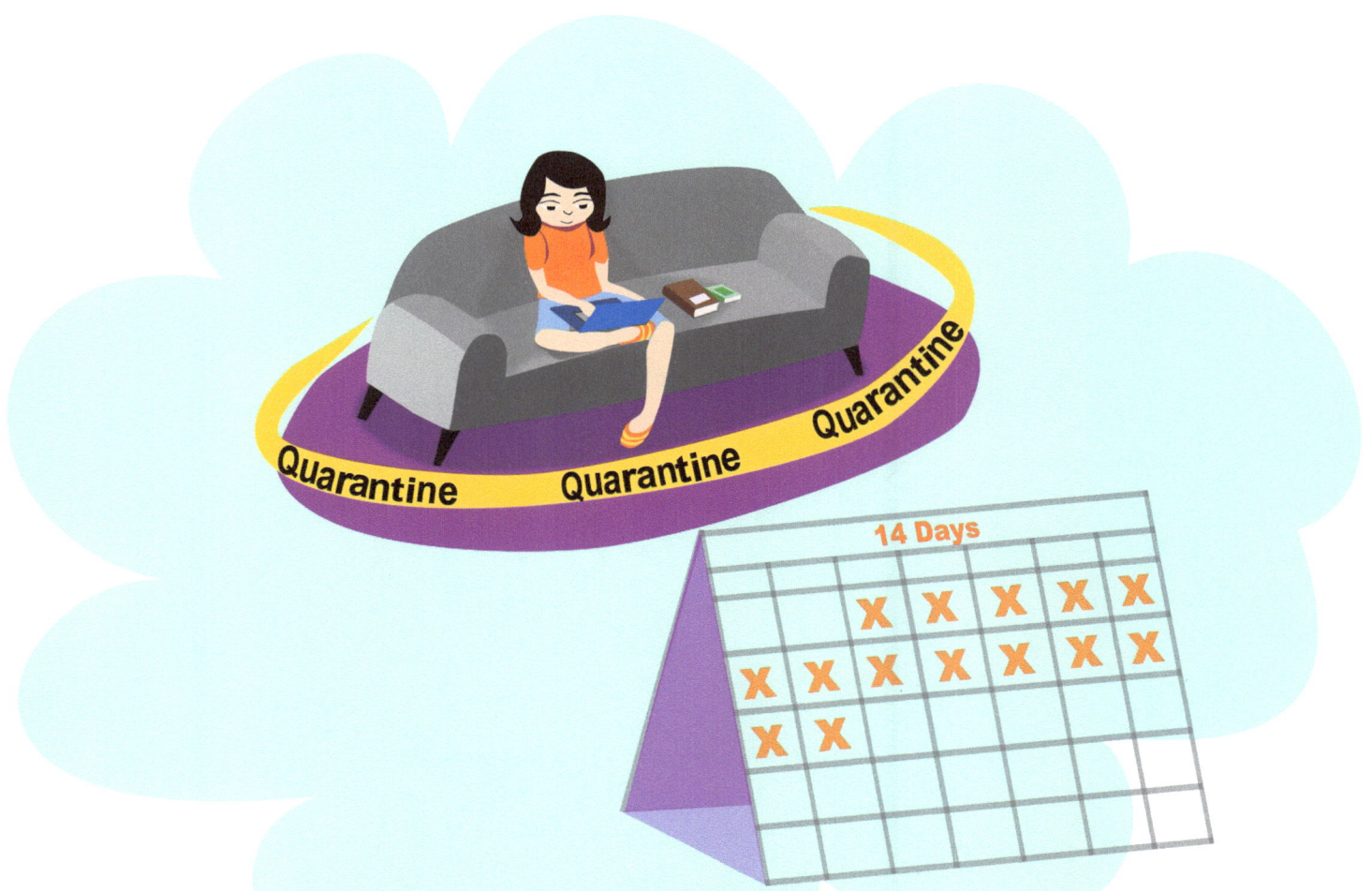

14 Days

In early December of 2019, Dr. Fauci and Dr. Birx have been telling people to get tested, stay home, wear a mask when they are in public, and practice social distancing. This means to stand 6 feet away from people. Many people still contracted the virus, and some even died.

Playground
Closed

Why?

People around the world must practice safety responsibilities like wearing a mask in public and washing their hands after touching surfaces.

Anyone can catch Covid-19, regardless of their age. Anyone who gets this virus can become extremely ill and possibly die. Covid-19 affects everyone differently, and that is what makes this virus scary and unpredictable.

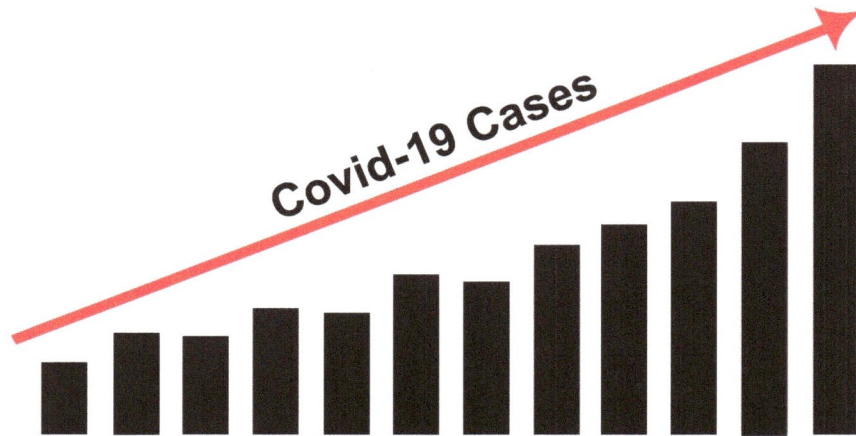

Covid-19 Cases

Every state counts the number of positive cases of Covid-19 daily. If the numbers continue to rise and not go down, the governor of that state must alert citizens. Most times precautions and restrictions are imposed, like closing amusement parks, schools for face-to-face teaching, and public pools. These places and more will be closed until the state's Covid-19 positive cases have decreased.

21

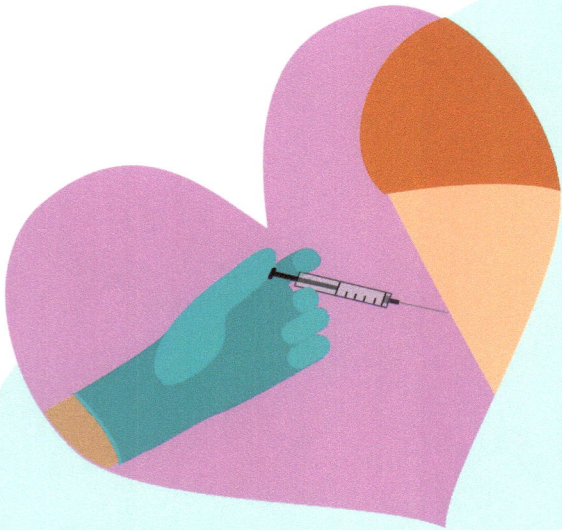

Three vaccines have been developed and tested since the outbreak of COVID-19. All three vaccines are 100% effective in preventing severe Covid-19 symptoms. The companies responsible for the vaccines are Pfizer-BioNTech, Moderna, and Johnson & Johnson. Millions of people have taken one of the three vaccines while millions of others have sadly succumbed to the complications of Covid-19. States and countries throughout the world have begun to reopen. However, they have done so with restrictions and mask requirements. In the fall of 2021, schools reopened with the hope that things could be more normal. Students, teachers, and faculty had the opportunity to be face-to-face once again, resuming human connection, something we all need.

About the Author and Illustrators

Donna Johnson has been teaching in Florida over twenty years. Teaching primary students has always been her passion. During these unprecedented times of COVID-19, Donna believes strongly that students needed to learn hard facts about this pandemic.

Beverly Tunstall is an Illustrator, Artist and Designer. She grew up in Indianapolis, Indiana. At a young age, her teachers realized she was talented in drawing and painting. Beverly earned her degree in Graphic Design at Everest University, Orlando Florida. Her passion for illustrating children's books developed when she became a substitute teacher and reading mentor for high needs students in the public school system. She finds this line of work a true blessing and very rewarding.

Zoe Skogen is the granddaughter of the illustrator, Beverly Tunstall. Zoe likes to draw and do crafts. She has a good eye for color, design, and gives great advice from the perspective of a 6 year old. This was Zoe's contribution to the book.

More From the Author

If you enjoyed this book, please check out this other work by the author, Donna Johnson.

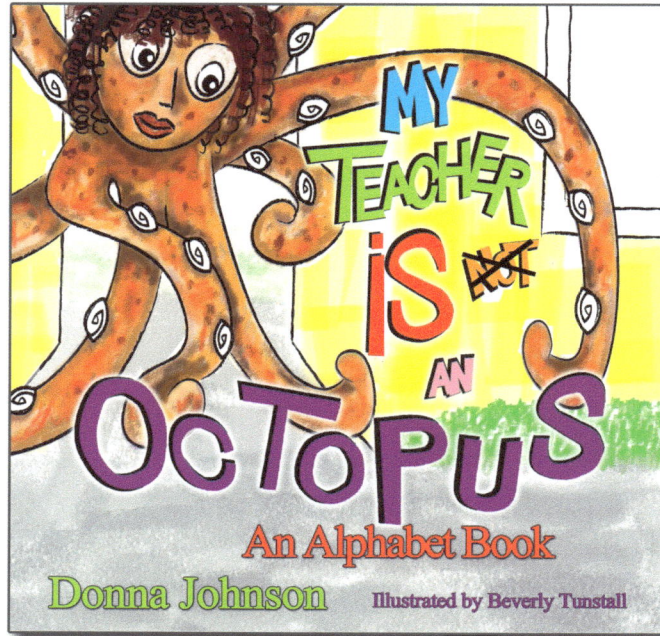

www.ingramcontent.com/pod-product-compliance
Lightning Source LLC
Chambersburg PA
CBHW060816090426

42737CB00002B/79